THE CLIMATE CRISIS IN
THE SOUTH

by Carollyne Hutter

FOCUS
READERS®

NAVIGATOR

WWW.FOCUSREADERS.COM

Focus Readers is distributed by North Star Editions:
sales@northstareditions.com | 888-417-0195

Produced for Focus Readers by Red Line Editorial.

Content Consultant: John Nielsen-Gammon, PhD, Regents Professor of Atmospheric Sciences, Texas A&M University

Photographs ©: Shutterstock Images, cover, 1, 7, 8–9, 12, 21, 27, 29; NASA Goddard/NOAA/NASA GOES Project/NASA, 4–5; Red Line Editorial, 10; Oliver de Ros/AP Images, 14–15; Eric Gay/AP Images, 17; Kathleen Flynn/Reuters/Alamy, 19; Rogelio V. Solis/AP Images, 22–23; US Coast Guard Atlantic Area/DVIDS, 25

Library of Congress Cataloging-in-Publication Data
Names: Hutter, Carollyne, author.
Title: The climate crisis in the South / Carollyne Hutter.
Description: Lake Elmo, MN : Focus Readers, [2024] | Series: The climate
   crisis in America | Includes index. | Audience: Grades 4-6
Identifiers: LCCN 2023002944 (print) | LCCN 2023002945 (ebook) | ISBN
   9781637396346 (hardcover) | ISBN 9781637396919 (paperback) | ISBN
   9781637397992 (pdf) | ISBN 9781637397480 (ebook)
Subjects: LCSH: Endangered ecosystems--Southern States--Juvenile
   literature. | Biodiversity--Climatic factors--Southern States--Juvenile
   literature.
Classification: LCC QH76.5.S69 H88 2024 (print) | LCC QH76.5.S69 (ebook)
   | DDC 577.27--dc23/eng/20230124
LC record available at https://lccn.loc.gov/2023002944
LC ebook record available at https://lccn.loc.gov/2023002945

Printed in the United States of America
Mankato, MN
082023

ABOUT THE AUTHOR

Carollyne Hutter writes for children and adults on science, geography, and the environment. She finds these fields fascinating and is always learning. She has written eight books and more than 25 magazine articles for children, covering such topics as the weather, rainforests, oceans, the arts, wildlife, and more.

TABLE OF CONTENTS

CHAPTER 1

HURRICANE HARVEY

In August 2017, Hurricane Harvey pounded the Texas coast. At landfall, Harvey's winds were more than 130 miles per hour (209 km/h). That speed made it a Category 4 hurricane. Then the storm weakened. But it still brought severe rains and **storm surges**.

A satellite image shows Hurricane Harvey on August 24, 2017.

Harvey stayed near Houston for days. Its heavy rainfall created harmful floods. One family woke up to find water rushing into their one-story house. The water soon rose to 4 feet (1.2 m) high. The family had to pack up and leave. They went two doors down to an empty raised home. They spent the night there to stay safe.

The next day, the water was lower. The family returned home. But their house was damaged. After Harvey, they tore down the old home. Then they built a new one much higher up.

Scientists believe **climate change** was one cause of Harvey's heavy rains.

Scientists think climate change increased Harvey's total rainfall by at least 7 percent, possibly much more.

Climate change is making the oceans warmer. Warm water is how storms get their energy. As a result, storms can create more powerful winds and heavier rain.

CHAPTER 2

CLIMATE OF THE SOUTH

Climate is different from weather. Climate describes an area's weather conditions over a long period of time. Weather describes how things are at a specific time. For instance, a desert might have a rainy day. That is an example of weather. But the desert's climate is still dry.

Cacti are able to grow in the dry climate of the South's deserts.

Kansas, Oklahoma, and Texas are part of the South. Arkansas, Louisiana, and Mississippi are, too. These states feature several climates. Western parts of the region tend to be dry. The Rocky

THE SOUTH

Mountains block moisture coming from the Pacific Ocean.

The rest of the South is wetter. The region receives moisture from the Gulf of Mexico. In fact, Mississippi, Louisiana, and Texas lie along the Gulf coast. This location often puts them in the path of hurricanes. Louisiana is the state that is most at risk of storm surges.

The South experiences a variety of extreme weather events. They include tornadoes, floods, hurricanes, and other storms.

Overall, summers are hot and **humid**. During humid weather, the air has more water in it. The air might feel moist.

A massive thunderstorm forms over the plains of Kansas.

Warmer air can hold more moisture than cooler air. This hot, humid air can rise into much cooler air above it. There, it forms storm clouds. For these reasons, summers in the South often have thunderstorms.

Winters in the South are mild. Most southern states do not get much cold weather or snow. But being farther north, Kansas can be a little different. It faces colder winters than the rest of the region.

INDIGENOUS FARMING

Indigenous peoples have farmed across the South for thousands of years. That includes the **ancestors** of the Caddo Nation. They once lived in Arkansas and Louisiana. They also lived in eastern parts of Oklahoma and Texas. People grew corn, squash, and bean crops near rivers. They also used **crop rotation**. This practice is better for the soil.

CHAPTER 3

IMPACTS ALREADY

Climate change is already affecting the South. Throughout the region, average temperatures are getting hotter. This rise has been greatest in Texas and Kansas. Heat waves are becoming more common and severe.

Temperatures in the South are already high. For this reason, even small

A Guatemalan mother mourns her son, who died trying to reach the United States. Border laws and the South's heat are often a deadly combination.

increases can cause serious harm. Too much heat can kill people. For example, between 2018 and 2021, the heat killed nearly 400 people in Texas.

Higher temperatures are also making droughts worse. Droughts are times of

CLIMATE AND ILLNESS

Climate change is making diseases more likely to spread. This change is already hitting the South. Warming temperatures are bringing new insects to the region. These insects typically live in the hot tropics. But now they can survive farther north. And they can carry viruses. In 2021, Texas had a warm winter. Mosquitoes carrying the West Nile virus came to the state. Hundreds of people in Texas got the virus. They were bitten by the mosquitoes.

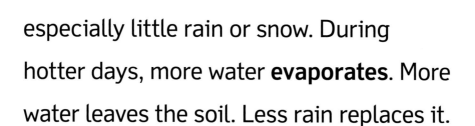

Cotton farms in Texas struggled because of the 2022 drought.

especially little rain or snow. During hotter days, more water **evaporates**. More water leaves the soil. Less rain replaces it.

Droughts affect farming and ranching. These industries are important in Kansas, Oklahoma, and Texas. Crops need rain to grow. Livestock feed on grasses, which need rain. As a result, droughts make it harder to farm and ranch.

Droughts are a major problem. But too much water is also a problem. Climate change is making tropical storms and hurricanes more intense. They often batter the coasts of Texas, Louisiana, and Mississippi.

Stronger storms do not solve droughts, either. Sometimes, most of the rain cannot soak into the ground fast enough. That extra water leads to more flooding. Areas near rivers are especially at risk of floods. Flooding can pollute water and damage buildings. It can also hurt people. In addition, parts of Louisiana are already below sea level. Those areas are at even higher risk of flooding.

Loss of wetlands and sea-level rise led the Biloxi-Chitimacha-Choctaw tribe to leave their Louisiana land.

Coastal areas of the South face another crisis. Climate change is one cause of rising sea levels. Rising sea levels can wash away homes and natural areas. People in some communities are already being forced to find new places to live.

BISON AND THE OKLAHOMA PRAIRIES

Tens of millions of bison once roamed the grasslands of North America. They provided food for Indigenous peoples. Then European settlers came. Many killed bison for sport. US settlers nearly wiped out the bison. By 1900, only a few hundred remained.

Since then, people have helped bison recover. In the 2020s, bison numbered in the hundreds of thousands. Indigenous nations are playing a key role in this work. There are several in Oklahoma.

Bison are helping restore Oklahoma's grasslands. The bison slowly eat the prairie grasses. They eat many types of grasses. As a

A bison grazes in a wildlife reserve in Oklahoma.

result, they can prevent one type of grass from taking over. This helps a variety of plants to grow. These plants are then eaten by many kinds of animals. The bison's work is helping grasses come back to the prairies. Other plants and animals have also returned. By helping the prairies, bison also help the climate. Grasslands are natural carbon sinks. This means they store more carbon than they release.

CHAPTER 4

TAKING ON CLIMATE CHANGE

People in the South can deal with the climate crisis in a number of ways. Slowing climate change is a key step. To do that, people must use fewer fossil fuels. These fuels are the major cause of climate change. They include coal, oil, and natural gas. Using them releases **greenhouse gases** into the atmosphere.

In 2021, nearly 75 percent of Mississippi's electricity came from natural gas.

Moving away from fossil fuels will be a challenge in the South. As in other areas, fossil fuels still meet much of the South's energy needs. The region is also a large producer of fossil fuels. Texas produces huge amounts of oil. Texas and Oklahoma are top producers of natural gas. Oil is also drilled in the Gulf of Mexico.

As a result, oil and gas are not just sources of energy. They are also big parts of the South's economy. Many people in the region depend on oil and gas jobs. In addition, the oil and gas industry is powerful. Like all industries, it focuses on profit. Using less fossil fuels means less money for oil and gas companies.

Fossil fuel production can be risky. In 2010, an explosion caused a massive oil spill in the Gulf of Mexico.

As a result, the industry often works to influence the South's politics. Its power has helped make sure leaders keep supporting oil and gas.

Even so, many people are working to help. For instance, more people concerned about climate action are running for political office. In addition, more oil and gas workers are supporting climate action. These groups can help shift the region away from fossil fuels.

Plus, parts of the South are already changing. Many places are shifting to **renewable energy**. Common renewable sources include the sun and wind. These power sources produce far less greenhouse gases than fossil fuels.

Much of the South is part of the Great Plains. As a result, it is very windy. That makes the region good for wind energy.

Kansas got nearly half of its electricity from wind power in 2021.

In fact, Texas, Kansas, and Oklahoma are leading states in wind power.

However, the climate crisis is already happening. For this reason, the region must also adapt to climate change. One important way is preparing for extreme weather. Cities are adapting by widening streams and waterways. They are fixing bridges. They are setting up better drainage systems. Also, many people are raising their homes. This way, their homes will be safer from flooding.

Restoring natural habitats can also help people adapt. Planting trees is one

REBUILDING COASTAL AREAS

Louisiana is at risk of rising sea levels. For this reason, the state is working to rebuild coastal wetlands. This project will protect people and businesses. It will also create new green jobs. More land along the coast will provide homes for animals. It will allow plants to grow. Wetlands also guard against strong storms. They absorb storm surges.

Wetlands are carbon sinks. They store more carbon than they release into the atmosphere.

example. Trees soak up carbon dioxide from the air. Across the South, people are experiencing climate change. The problems are serious. But many people in the region are working together to help.

FOCUS ON
THE SOUTH

Write your answers on a separate piece of paper.

1. Write a few sentences describing the main ideas of Chapter 3.

2. What are some extreme weather events you face where you live? How can your community adapt to those events?

3. Which state in the South is a leader in wind power?
- **A.** Arkansas
- **B.** Mississippi
- **C.** Texas

4. Why do parts of Louisiana, Mississippi, and Texas face more risk from rising sea levels?
- **A.** These states are covered by mountain ranges.
- **B.** These states have coastal areas.
- **C.** These states are entirely inland.

Answer key on page 32.

GLOSSARY

ancestors
Family members from the past.

climate change
Human-caused long-term changes in Earth's temperature and weather patterns.

crop rotation
The method of switching crops season to season on the same land.

evaporates
Changes from liquid to gas.

greenhouse gases
Gases that trap heat in Earth's atmosphere, causing climate change.

humid
Having a lot of moisture in the air.

Indigenous
Native to a region, or belonging to ancestors who lived in a region before colonists arrived.

renewable energy
Energy produced from a source that will not run out.

storm surges
Risings of the sea that are caused by storms' winds.

TO LEARN MORE

BOOKS

Gagne, Tammy. *Texas*. Minneapolis: Abdo Publishing, 2023.

Henzel, Cynthia Kennedy. *Using Carbon Sinks to Fight Climate Change*. Lake Elmo, MN: Focus Readers, 2023.

Huddleston, Emma. *Adapting to Climate Change*. Minneapolis: Abdo Publishing, 2021.

NOTE TO EDUCATORS

Visit **www.focusreaders.com** to find lesson plans, activities, links, and other resources related to this title.

INDEX

Answer Key: 1. Answers will vary; **2.** Answers will vary; **3.** C; **4.** B